People Need People

Benjamin Zephaniah • Nila Aye

ORCHARD

To walk to
To talk to
To cry and rely on,
People will always need people.

For the people who came before us
from far across the sea.
For the great people who built this land
people like my mummy.

B.Z.

Dedicated to all.
We are all people, we are all the same.
Let's work together to make a better world.

N.A.

ORCHARD BOOKS
Text first published in Great Britain in 2000
in *Wicked World* by Puffin Books

This edition first published in hardback in 2022
by Hodder and Stoughton

First published in paperback in 2023

1 3 5 7 9 10 8 6 4 2

Text © Benjamin Zephaniah, 2000
Illustrations © Nila Aye, 2022

The moral rights of the author and illustrator have been asserted.
All rights reserved.

A CIP catalogue record for this book is available
from the British Library.

HB ISBN 978 1 40836 815 2
PB ISBN 978 1 40836 816 9

Printed and bound in China

MIX
Paper from
responsible sources
FSC
www.fsc.org
FSC® C104740

Orchard Books
An imprint of Hachette Children's Group
Part of Hodder and Stoughton
Carmelite House, 50 Victoria Embankment,
London EC4Y 0DZ

An Hachette UK Company
www.hachette.co.uk
www.hachettechildrens.co.uk

Departures
Arrivals

←1-11 | 12-23→

To love and to miss
To hug and to kiss,
It's useful to have other people.

-20%

-20%

To whom will you moan
If you're all alone,
It's so hard to share
When no one is there.

There's not much to do
When there's no one but you.
People will always need people.

To please
To tease
To put you at ease,
People will always need people.

To make life appealing
And give life some meaning,
It's useful to have other people.

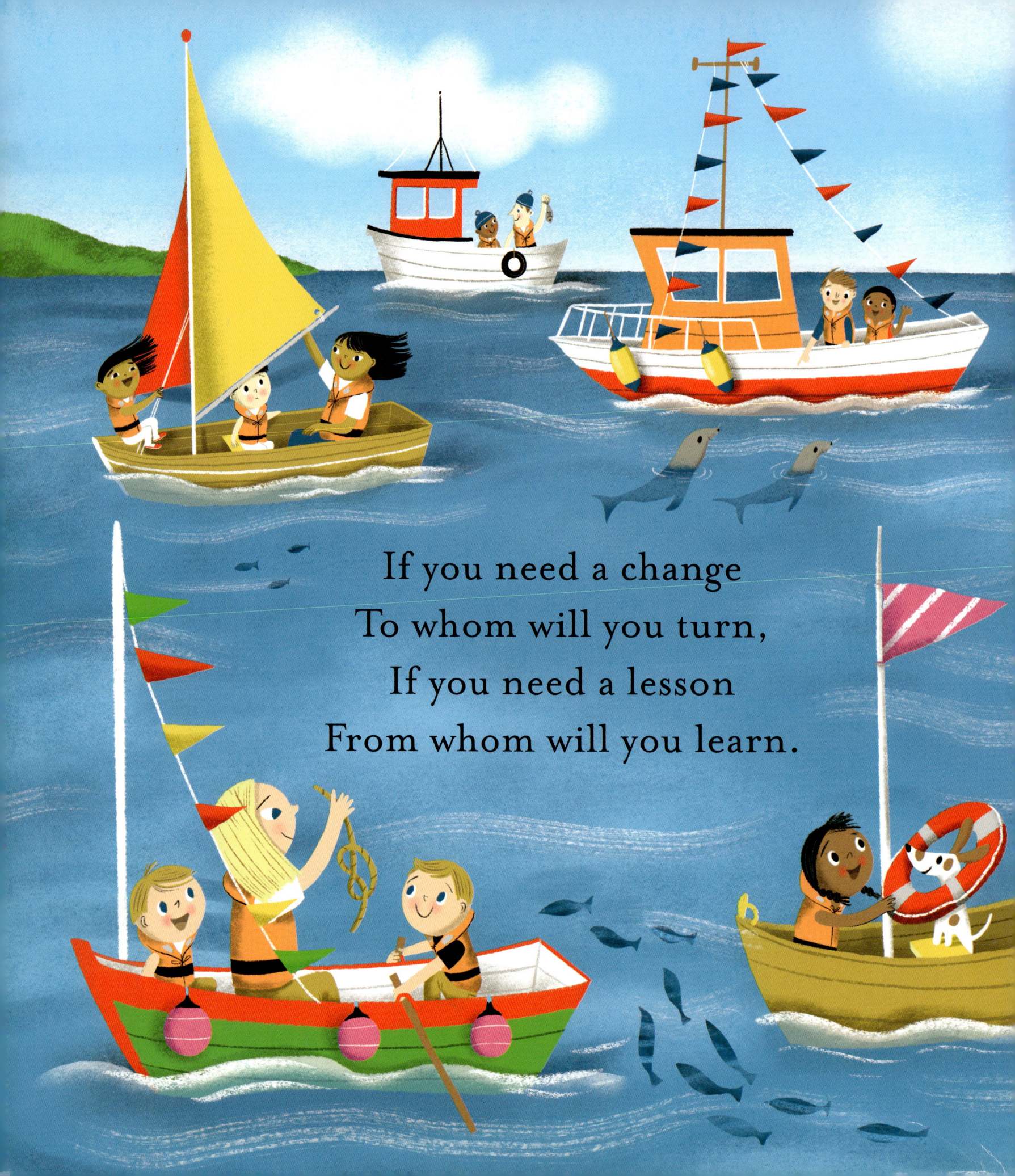

If you need a change
To whom will you turn,
If you need a lesson
From whom will you learn.

If you need to play
You'll know why I say
People will always need people.

As girlfriends
As boyfriends
From Mumbai
To Ostend,
**People will always
need people.**

To have friendly fights with
And share tasty bites with,
It's useful to have other people.

People live in families
Gangs, posses and packs,
It seems we need company
Before we relax . . .

LOVE

So stop making enemies
And let's face the facts,

People will always need people.

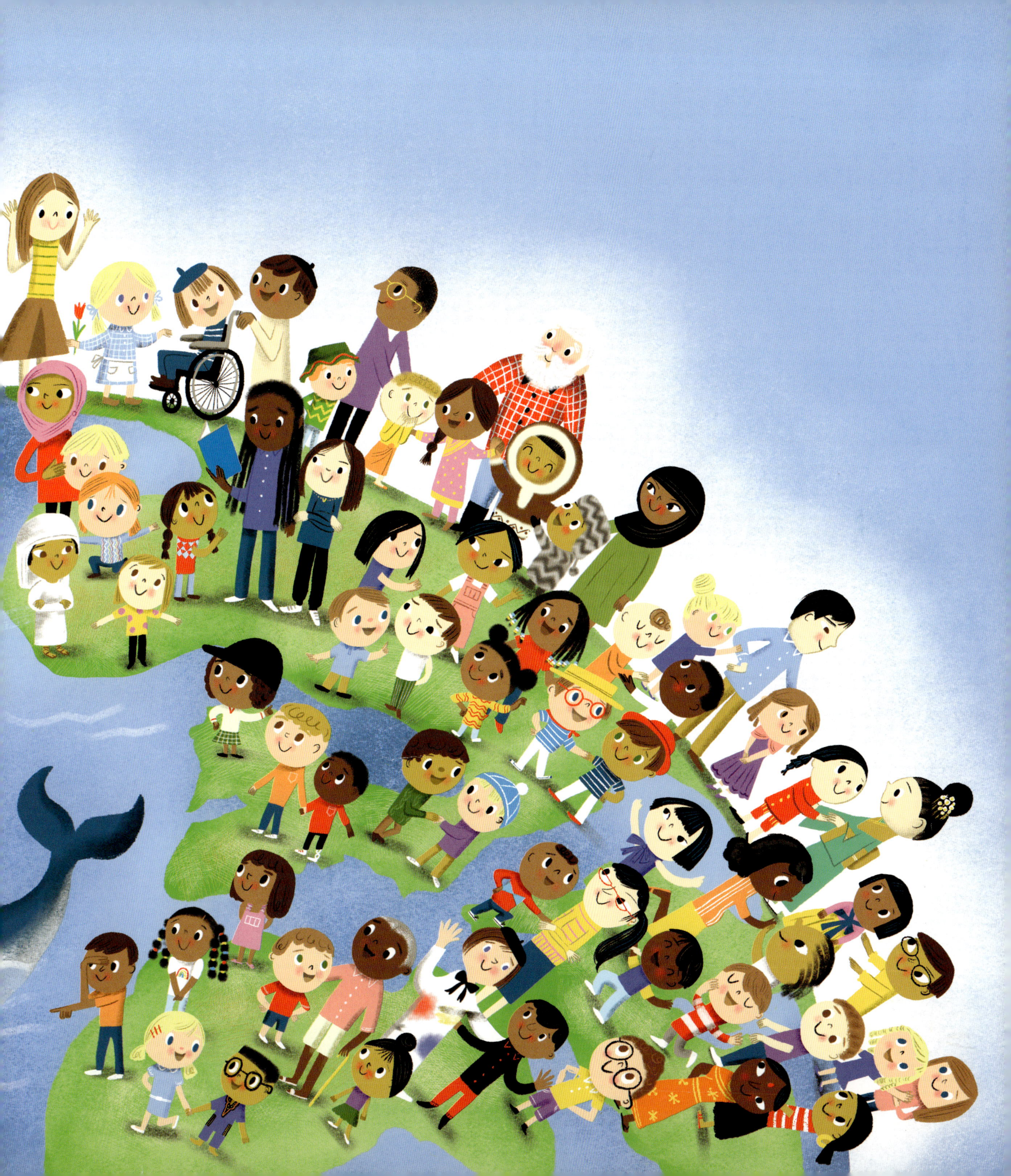

Oh yes,
People will always need people.

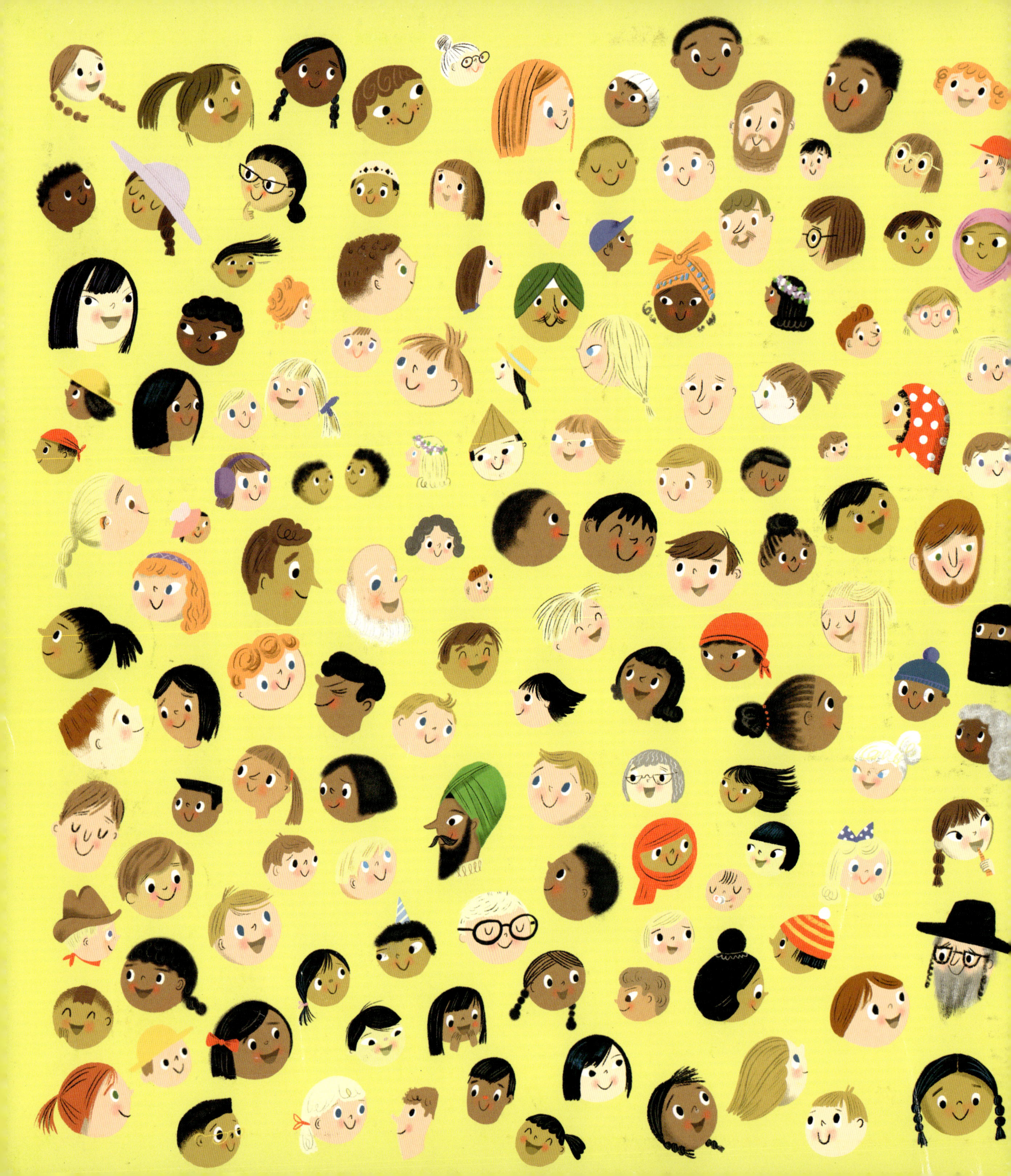